Color Free Adult Coloring Book: Encouraging and Inspirational Phrases

BY: CATHY J POPE

HEY FRIENDS!

PLEASE ENJOY 30 PAGES OF AWESOME,

INSPIRATIONAL, AND ENCOURAGING

COLOR FREE CREATIONS!

EACH PAGE IN THIS COLOR FREE ADULT COLORING BOOK IS PRINTED ONE-SIDED;

SO TEAR OUT, FRAME, AND HANG OR JUST ENJOY YOUR CREATIONS

WITHOUT DISTURBING THE OTHER PAGES!

© 2017 CATHY J POPE. ALL RIGHTS RESERVED.

NO PART OF THIS BOOK MAY BE REPRODUCED OR TRANSMITTED BY ANY FORM OR BY ANY MEANS, ELECTRONICALLY OR MECHANICAL, INCLUDING PHOTOCOPY, RECORDING, OR ANY INFORMATION STORAGE OR RETRIEVAL SYSTEM, WITHOUT PRIOR WRITTEN CONSENT FROM THE AUTHOR.

CONNECT WITH CATHY J POPE ON INSTAGRAM AT @CATHYJPOPELA
OR THE WEB AT WWW.CATHYJPOPE.COM !

*This first ever Color Free adult coloring book
is dedicated to Brenda,
who inspires me everyday.*

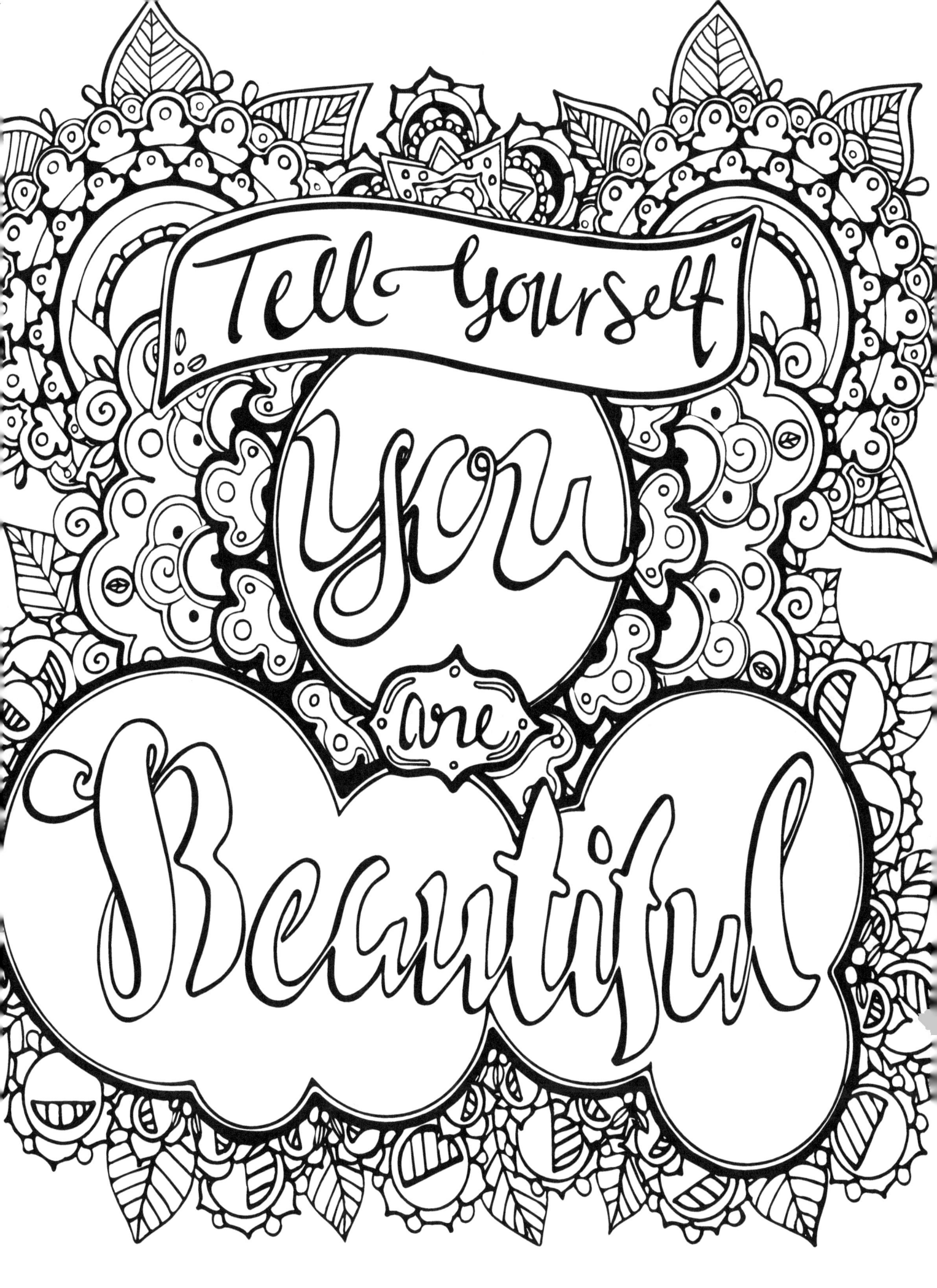

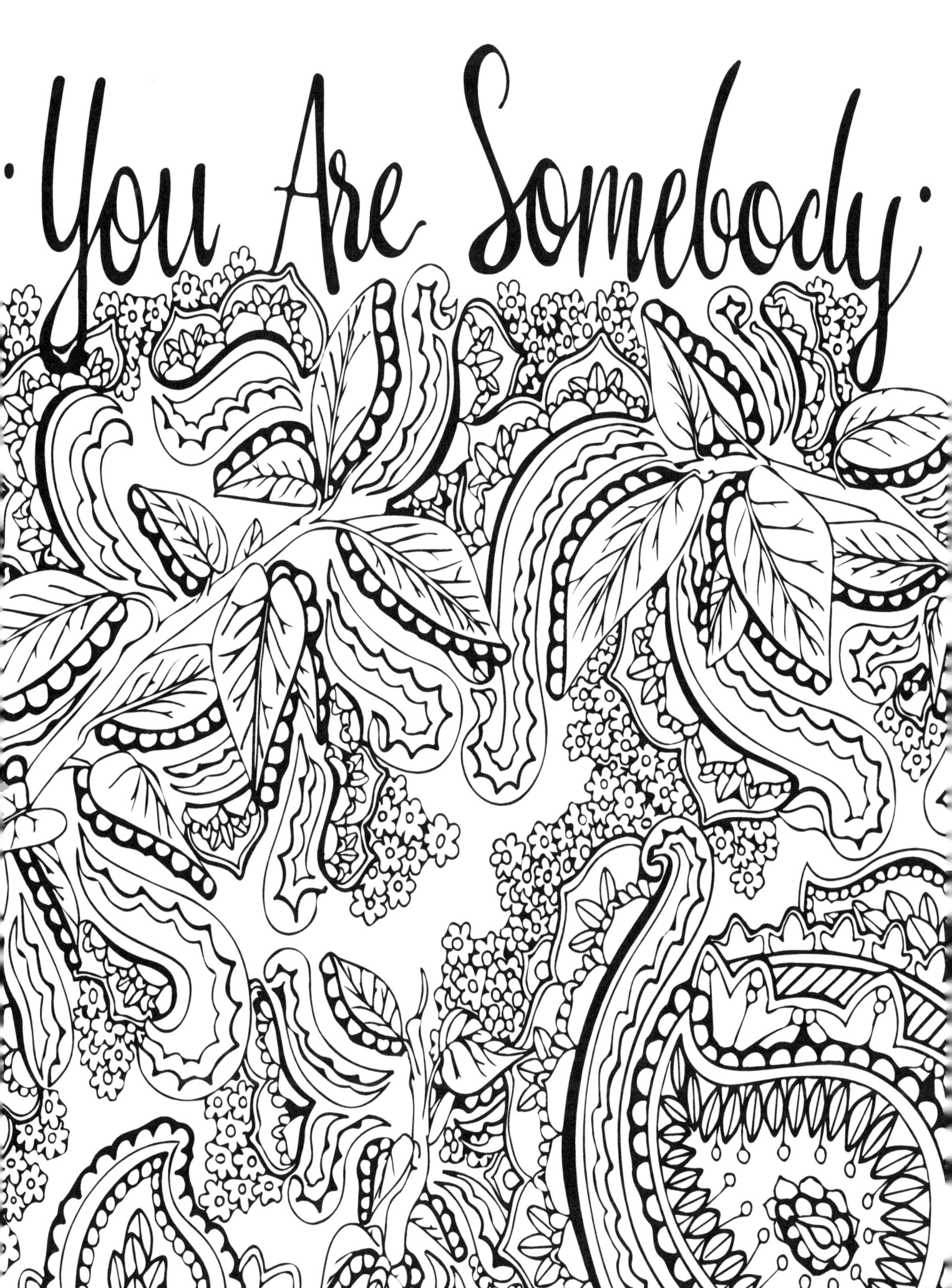

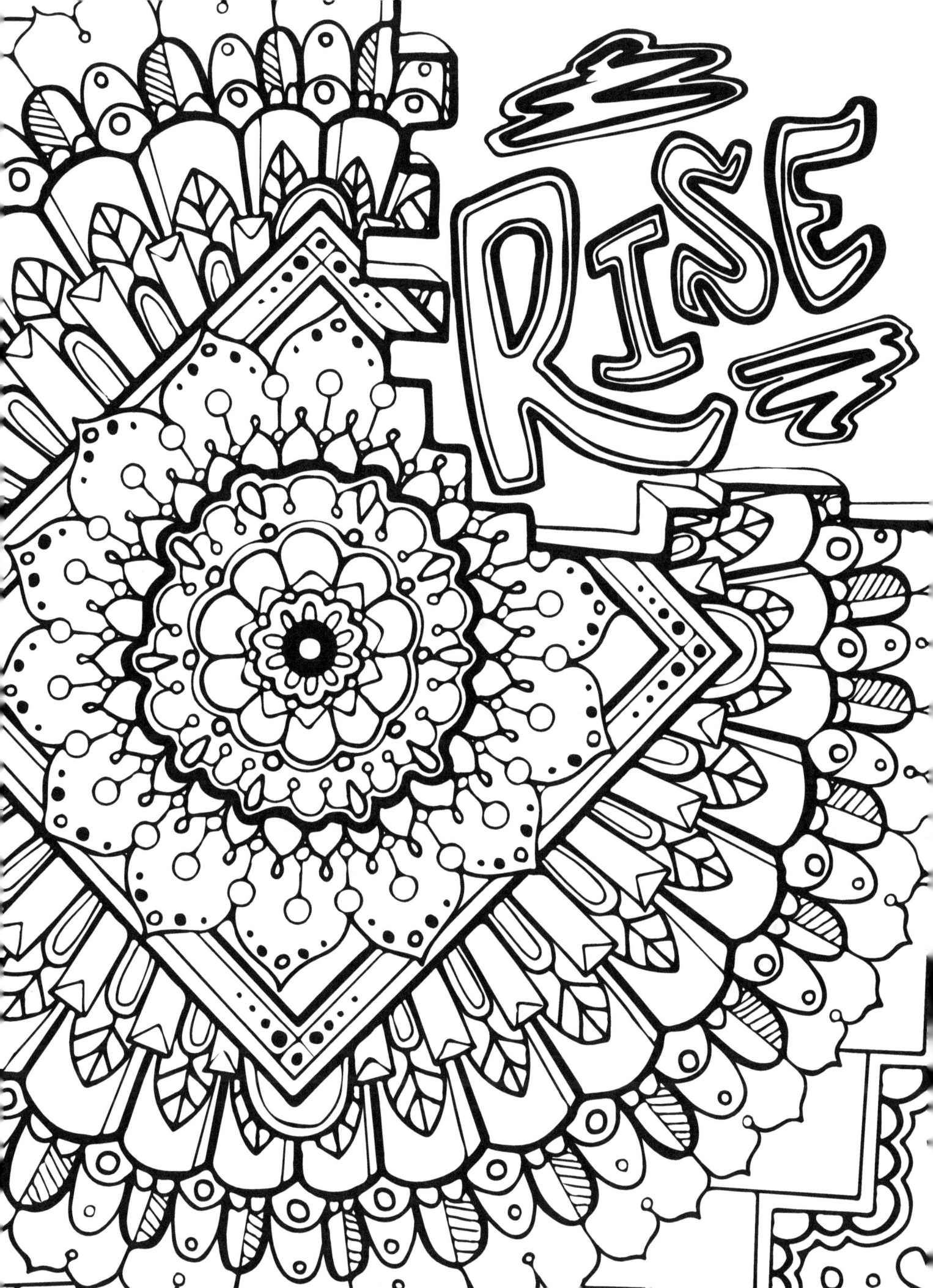

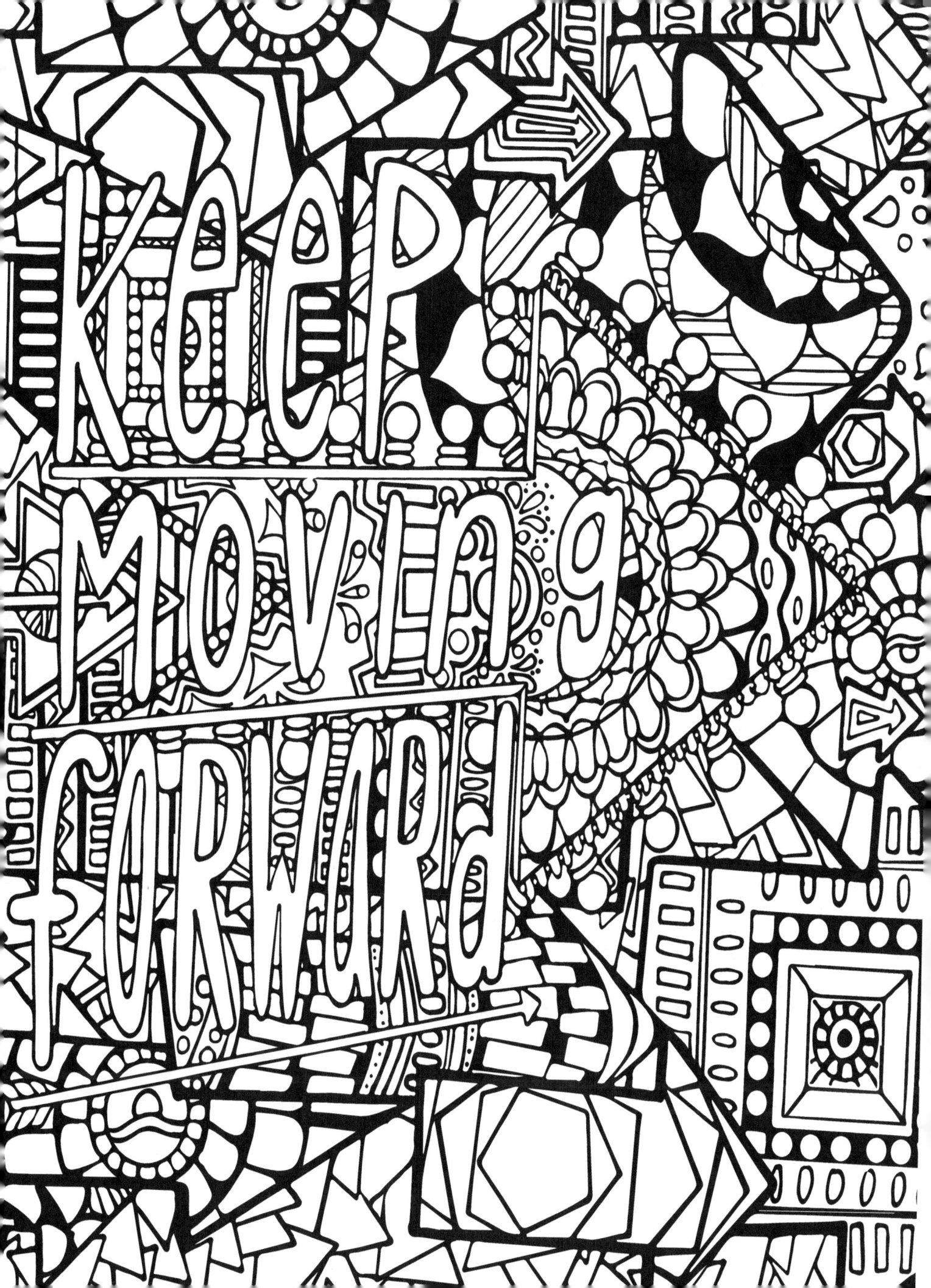

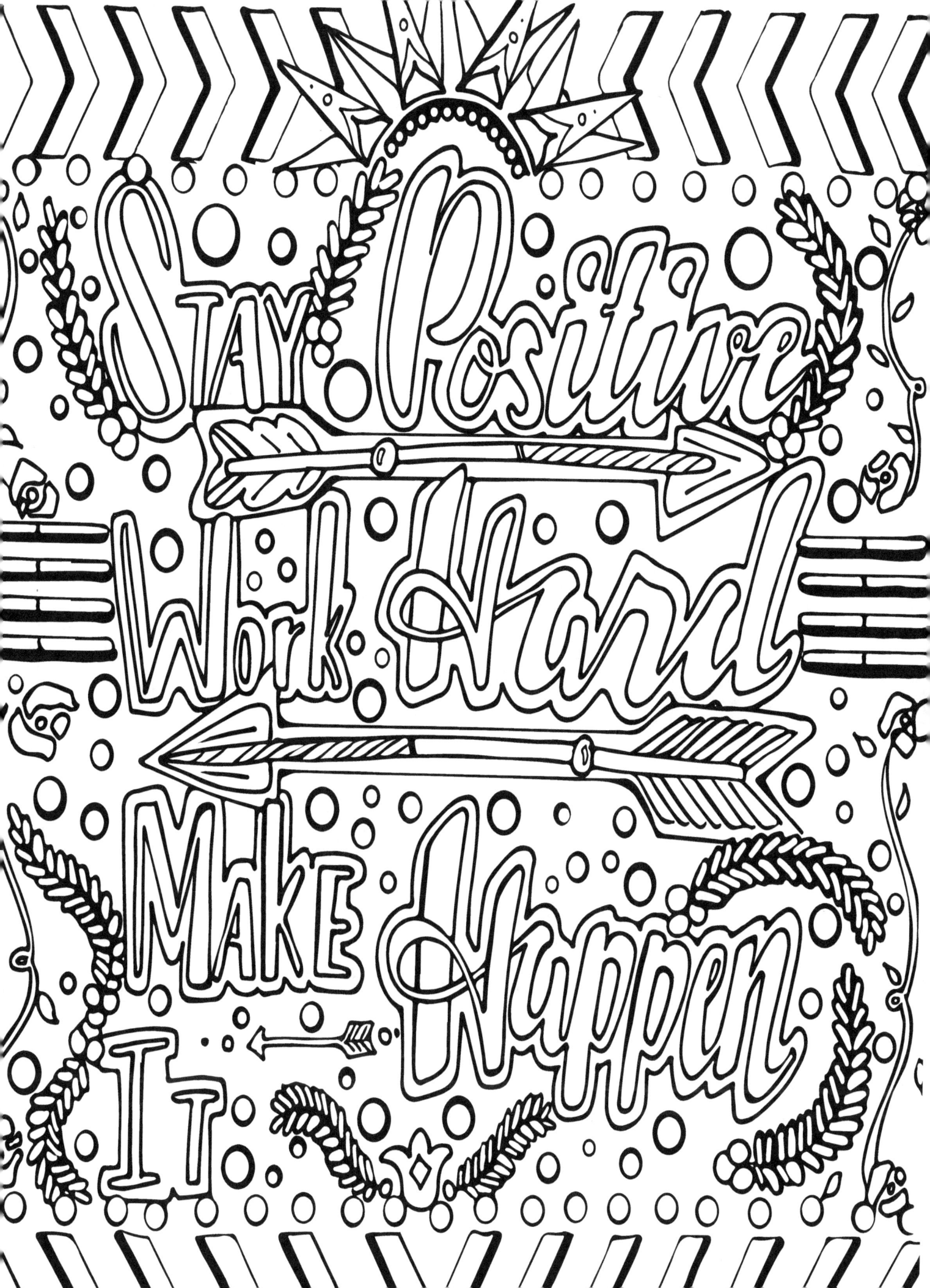

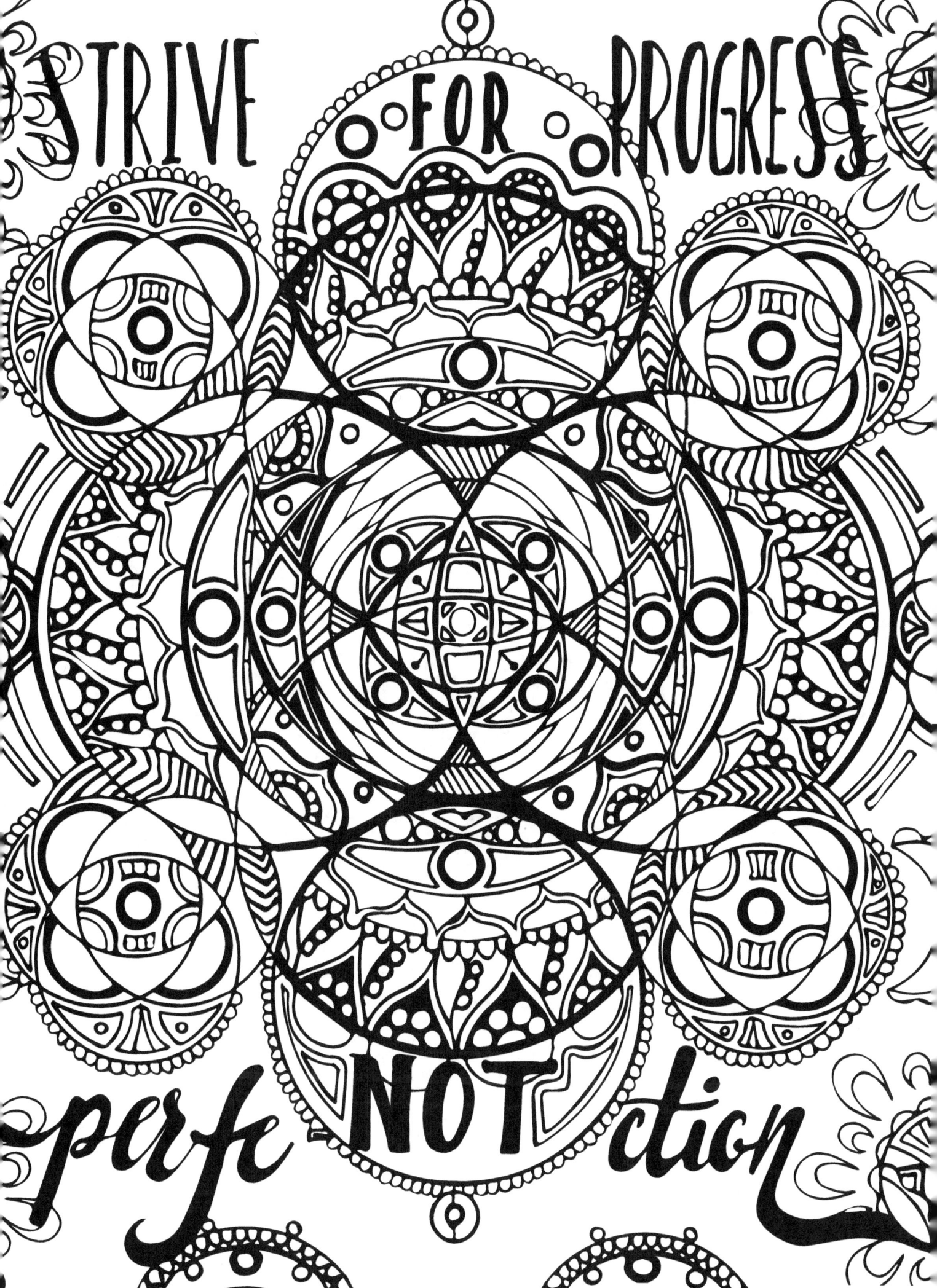

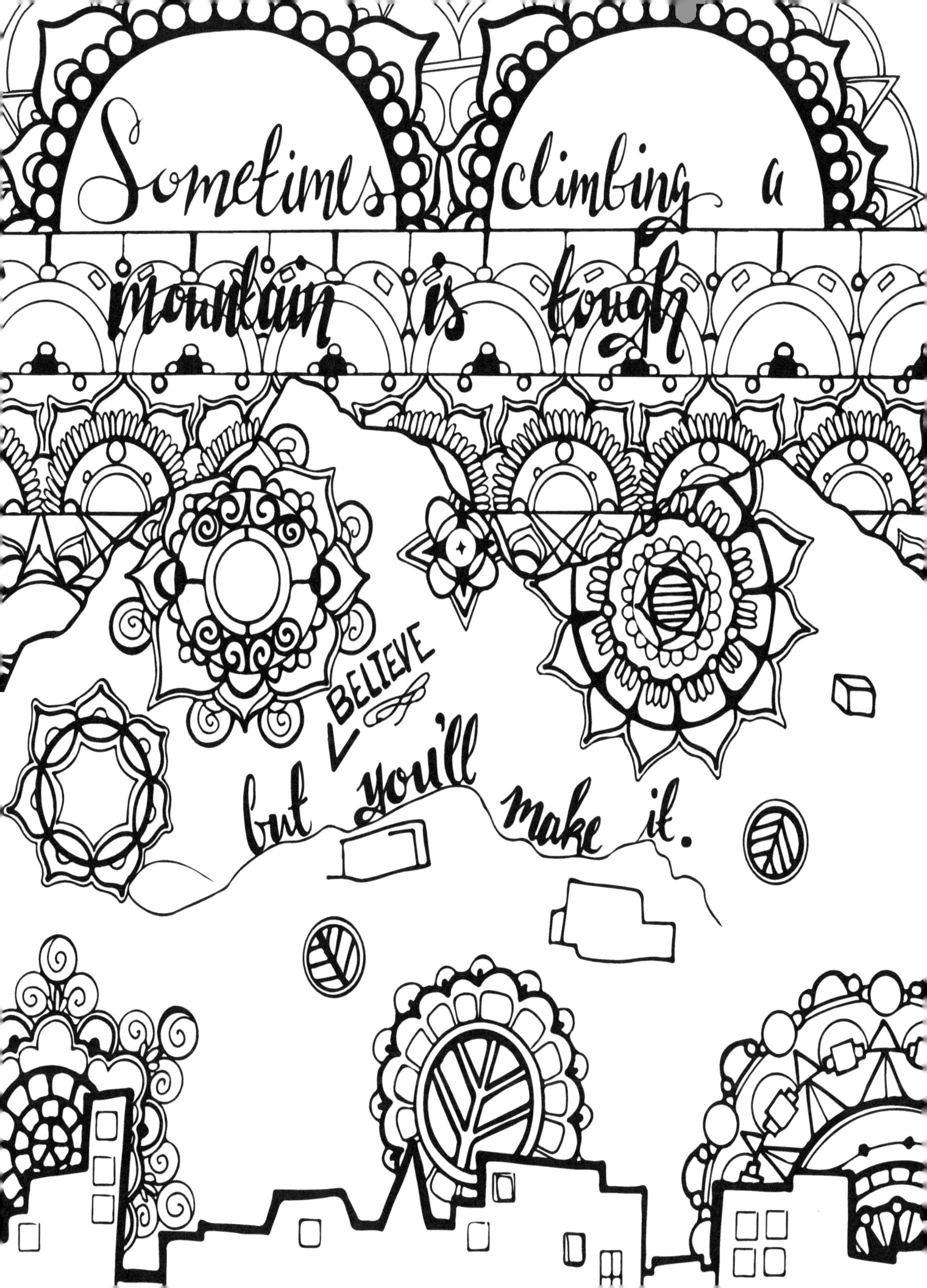

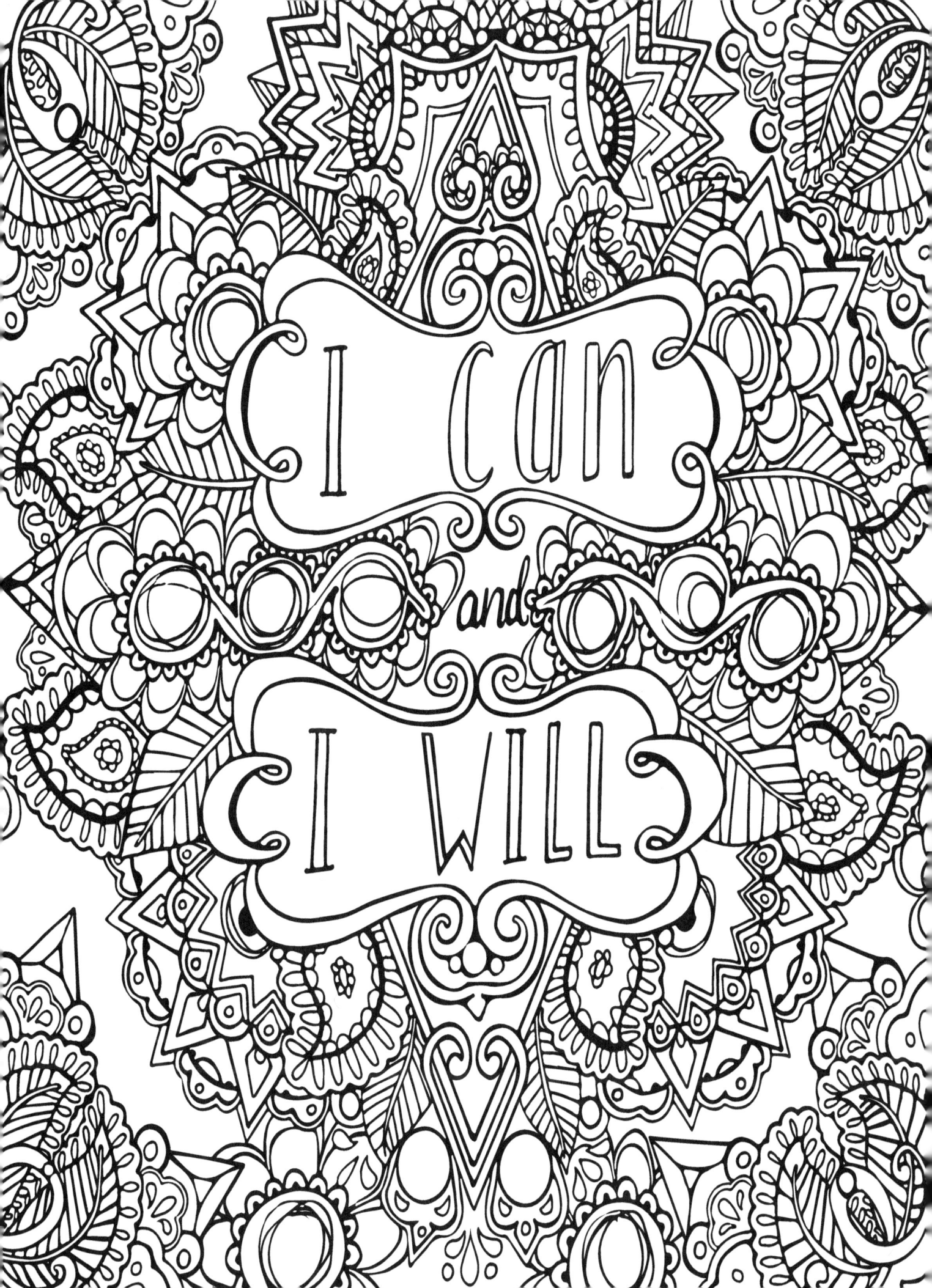

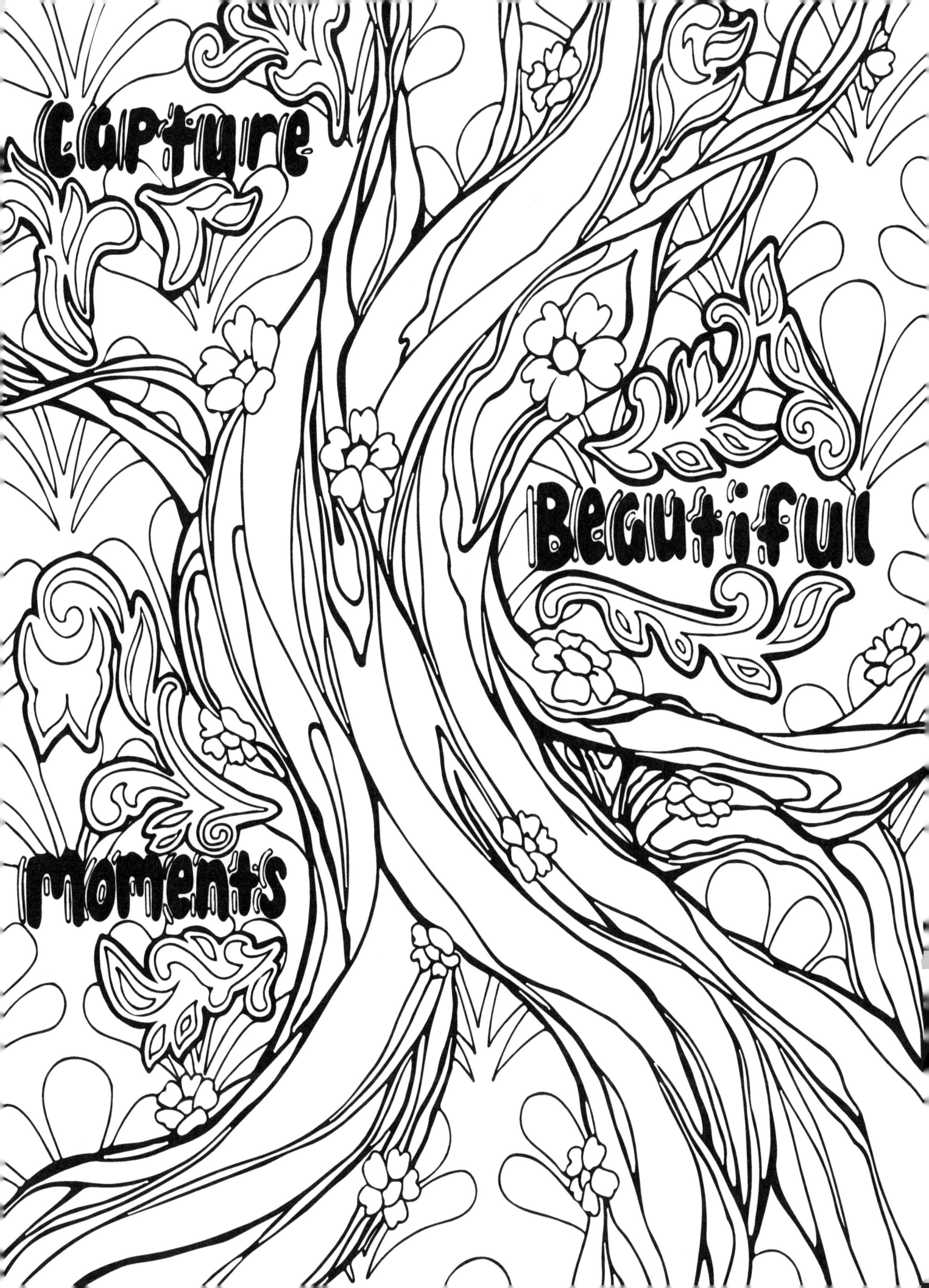

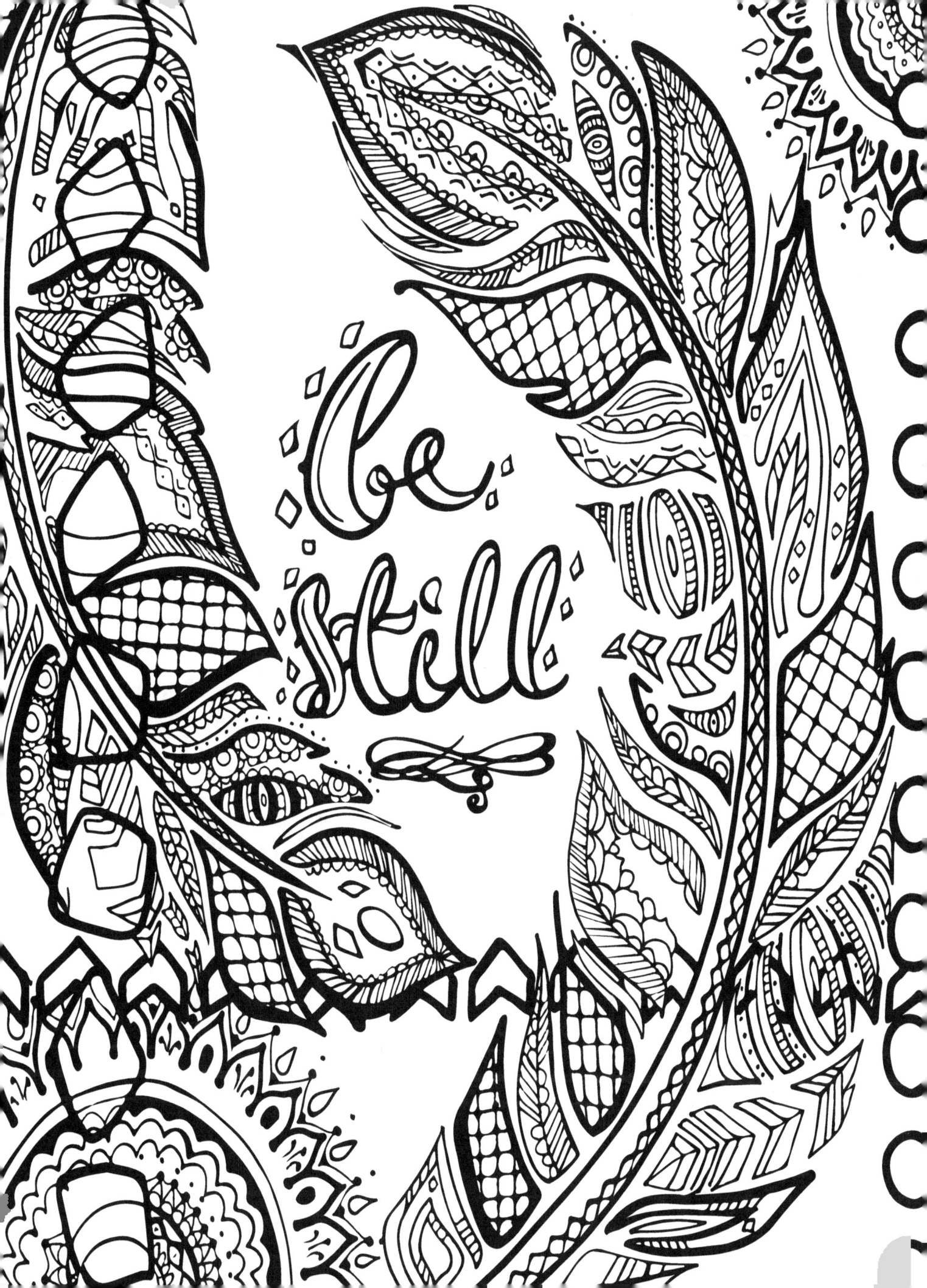

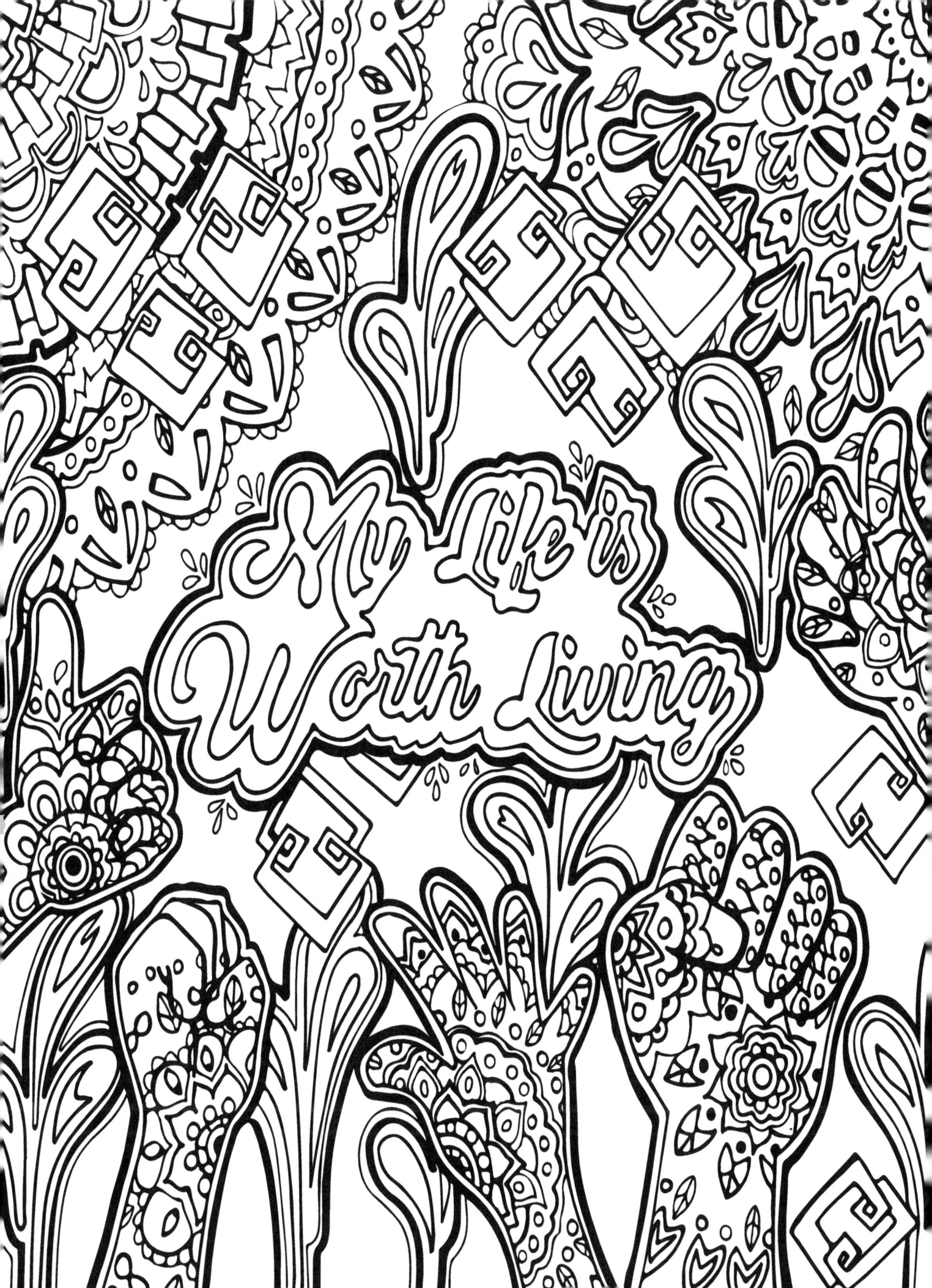

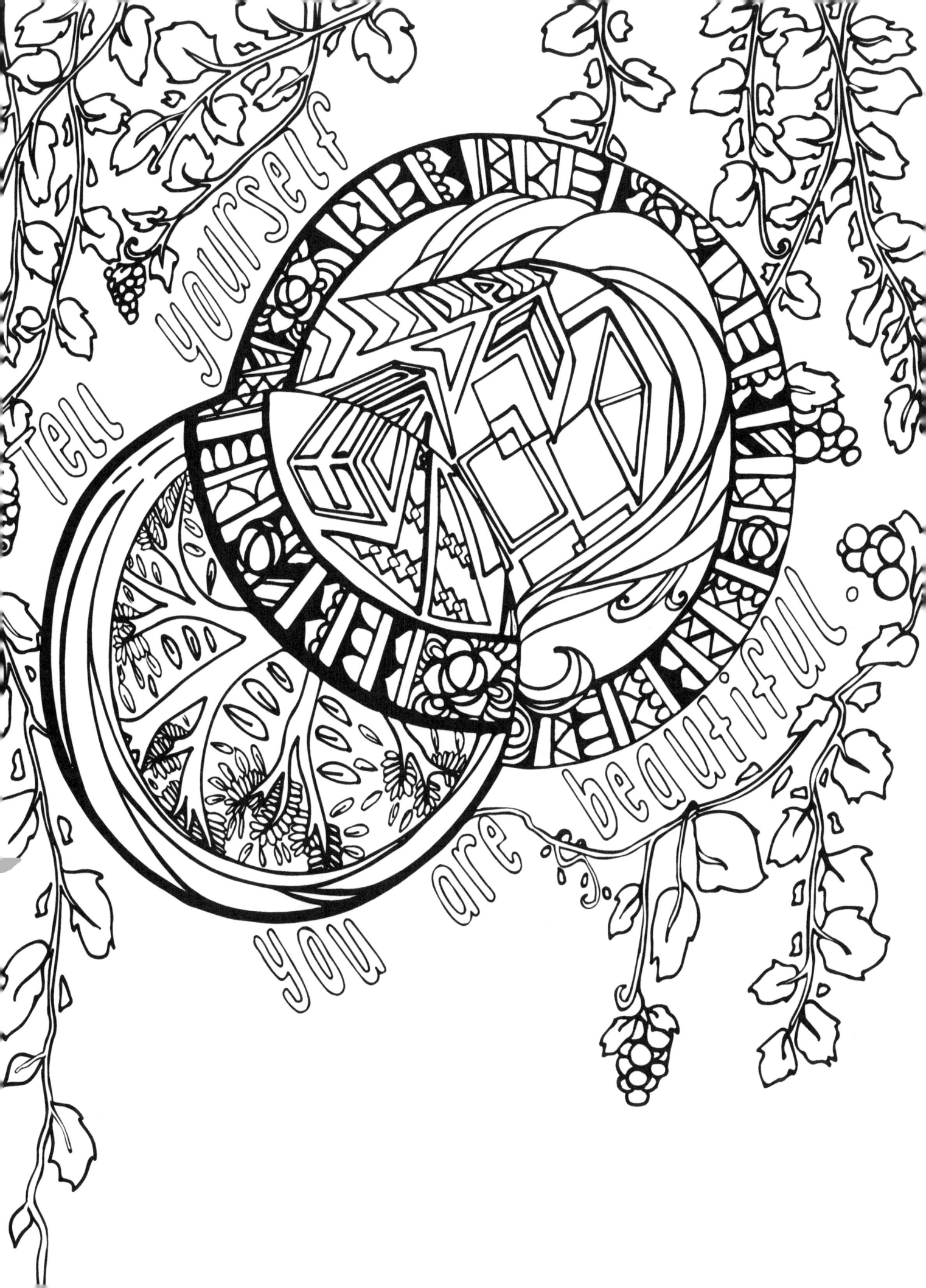

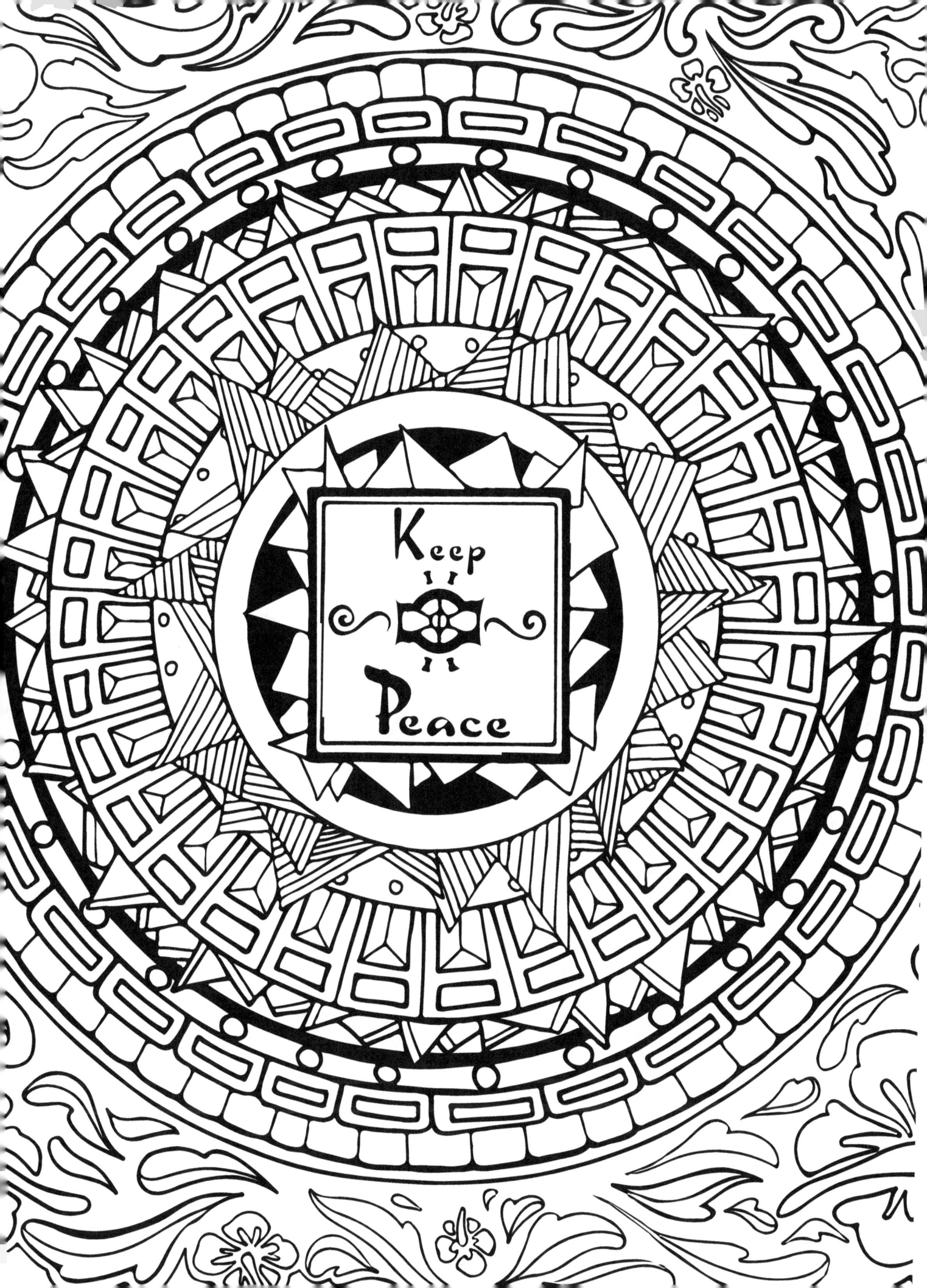

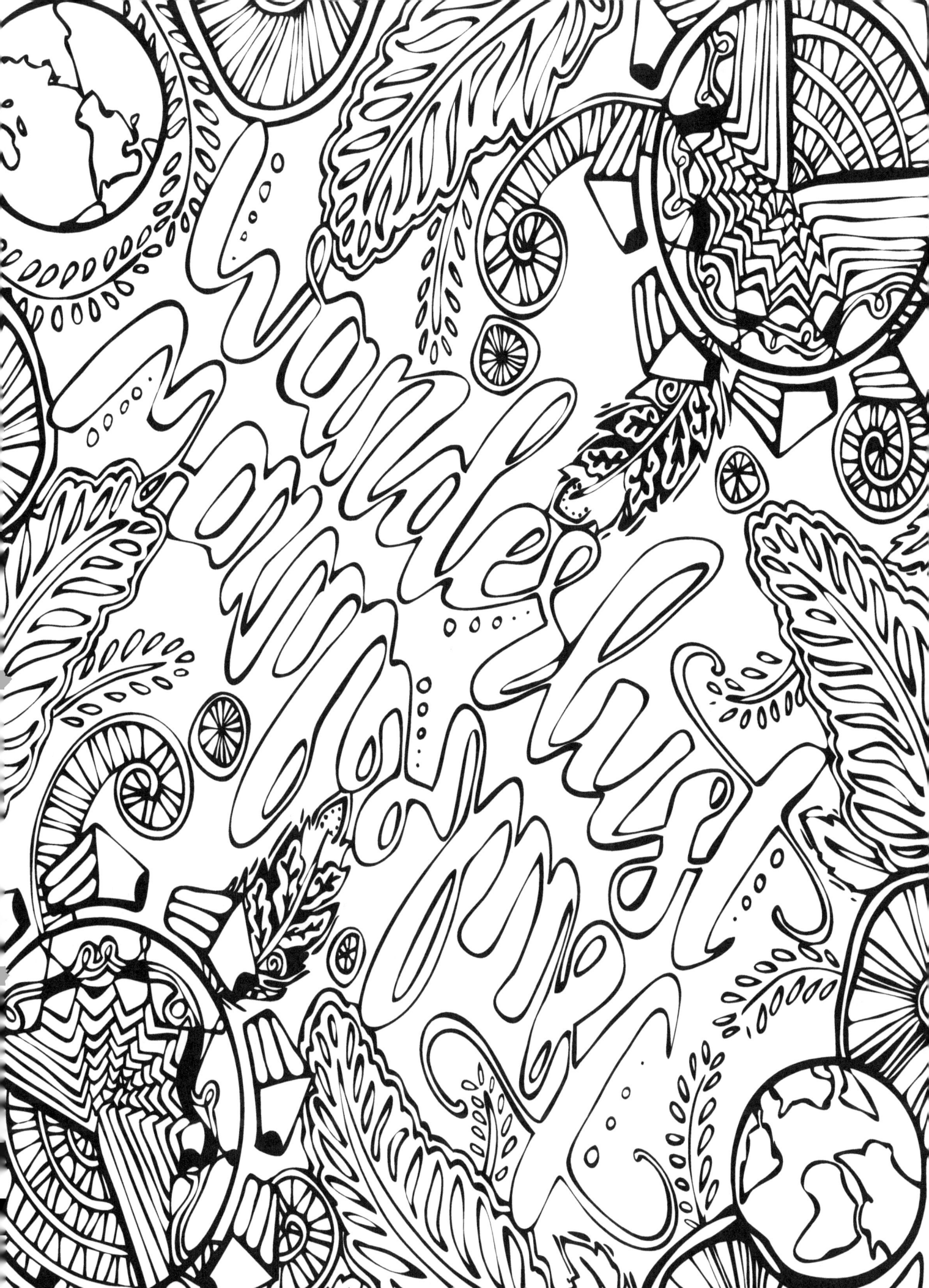

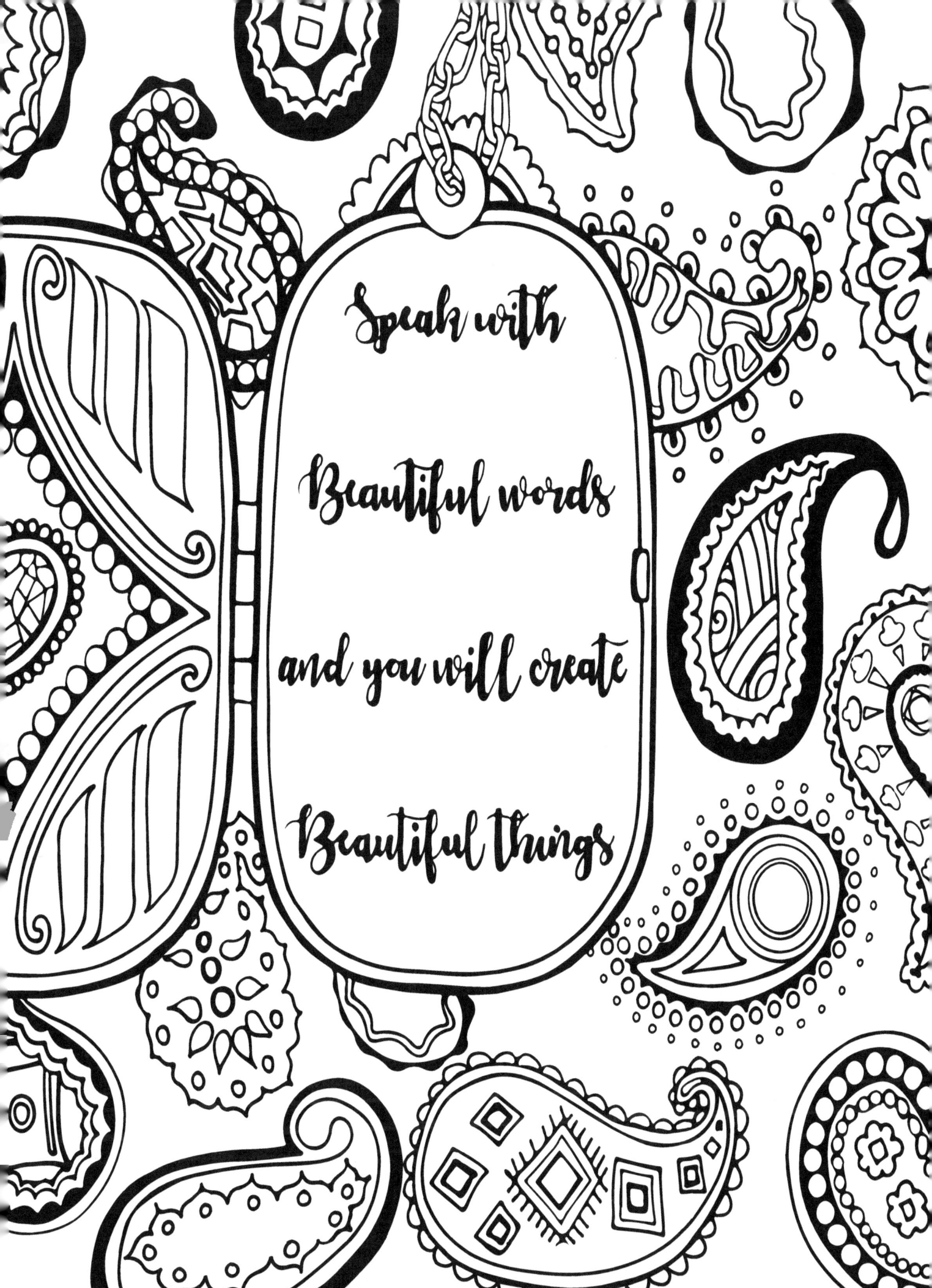

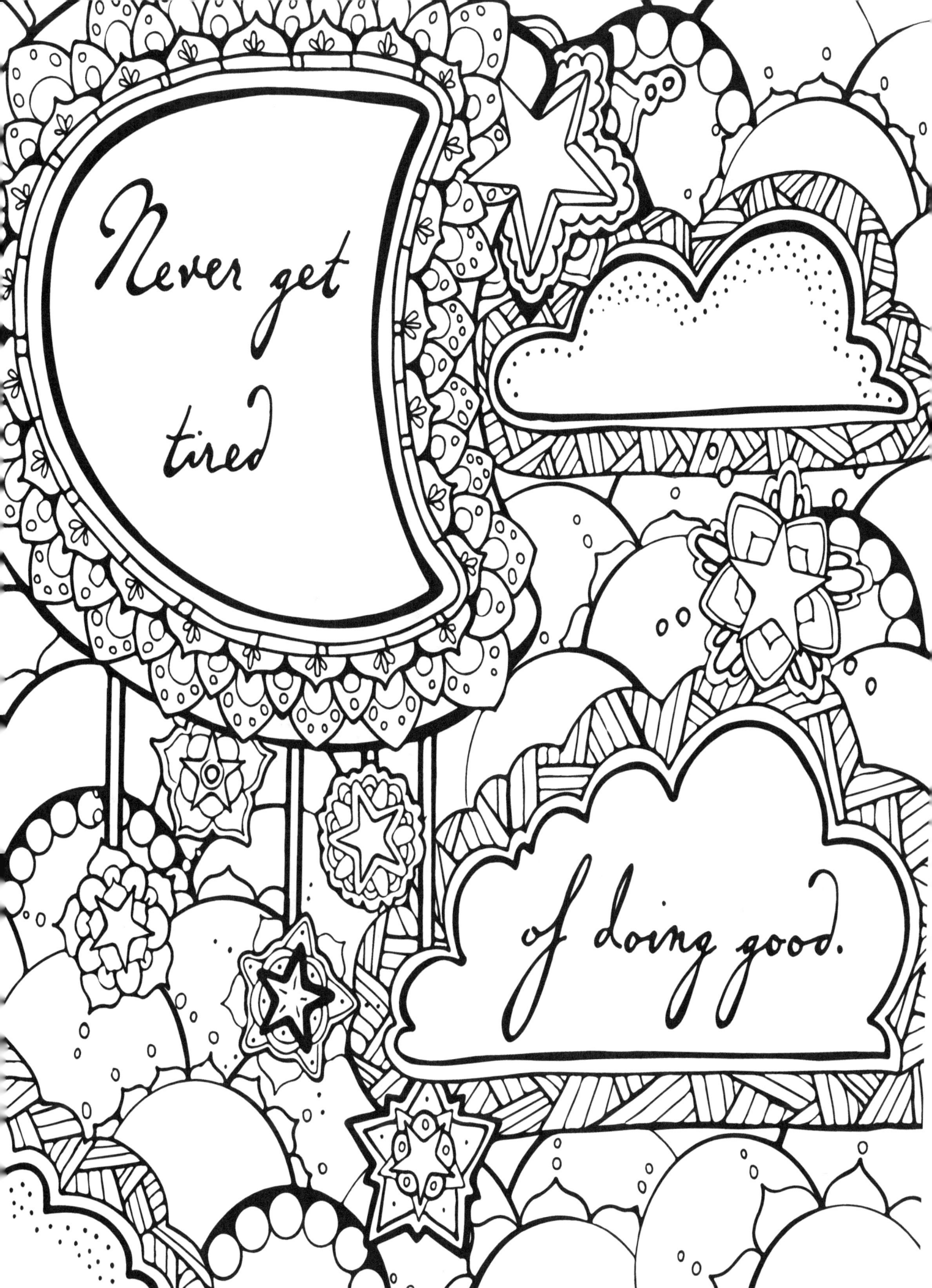

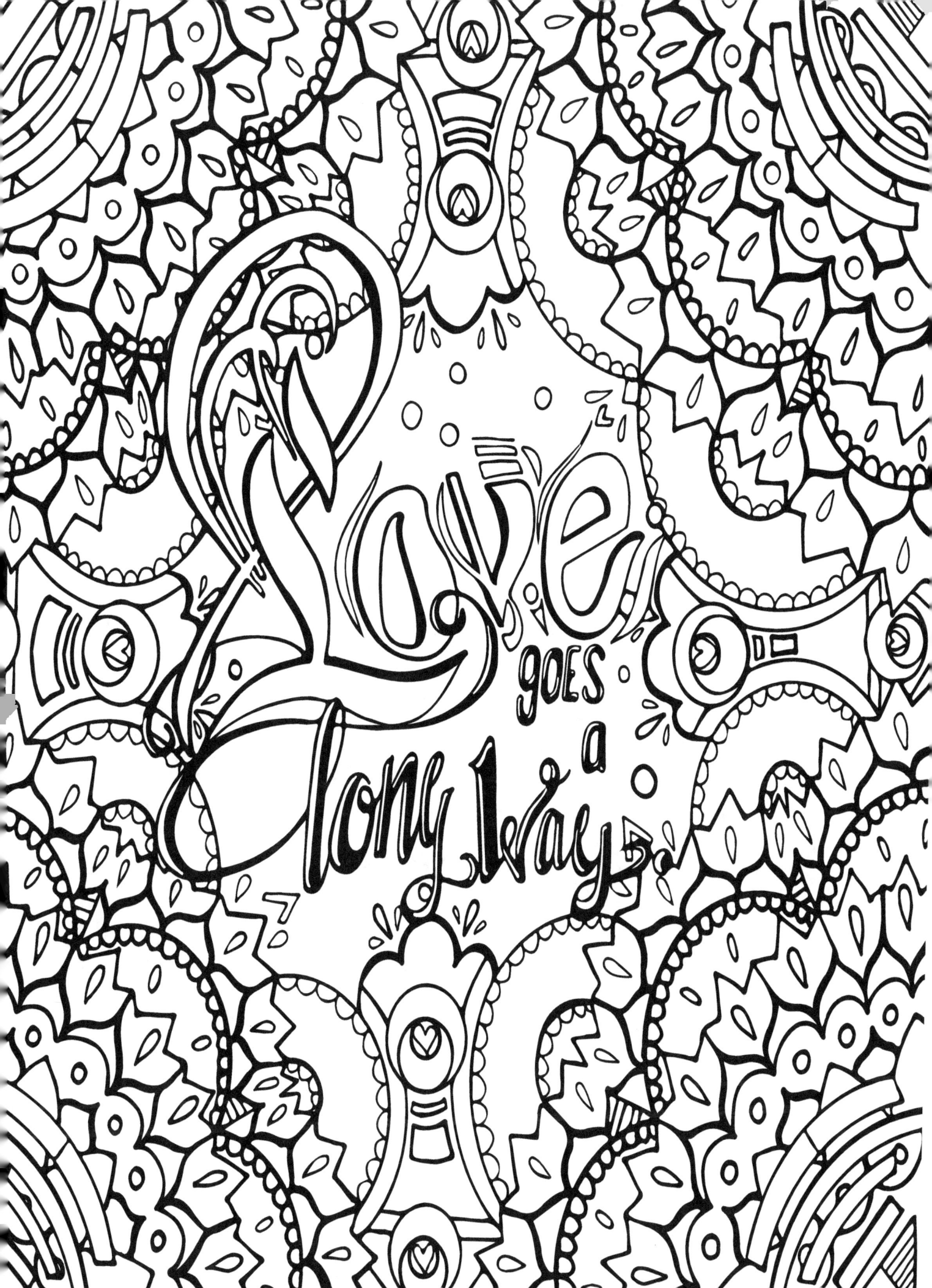

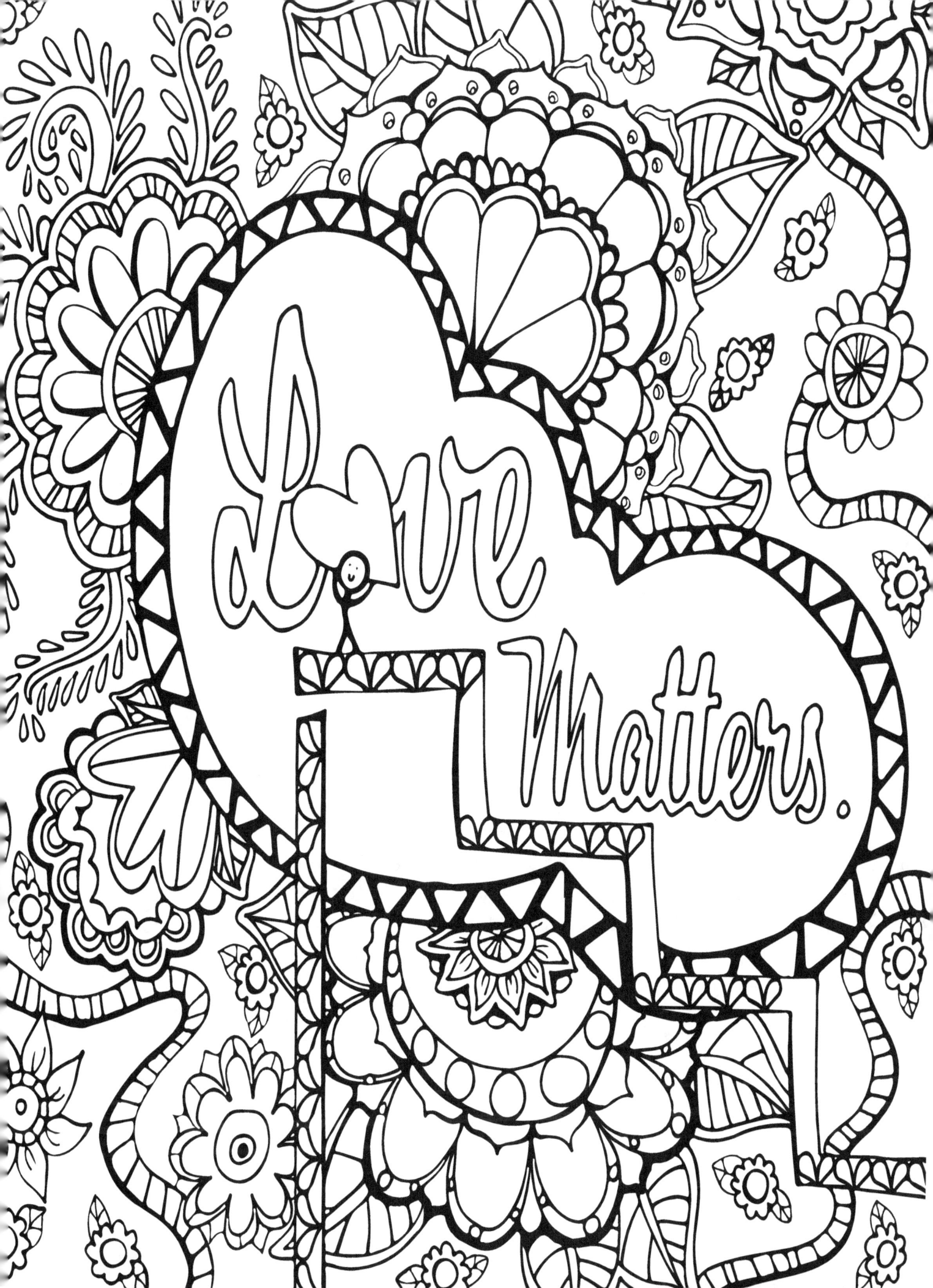

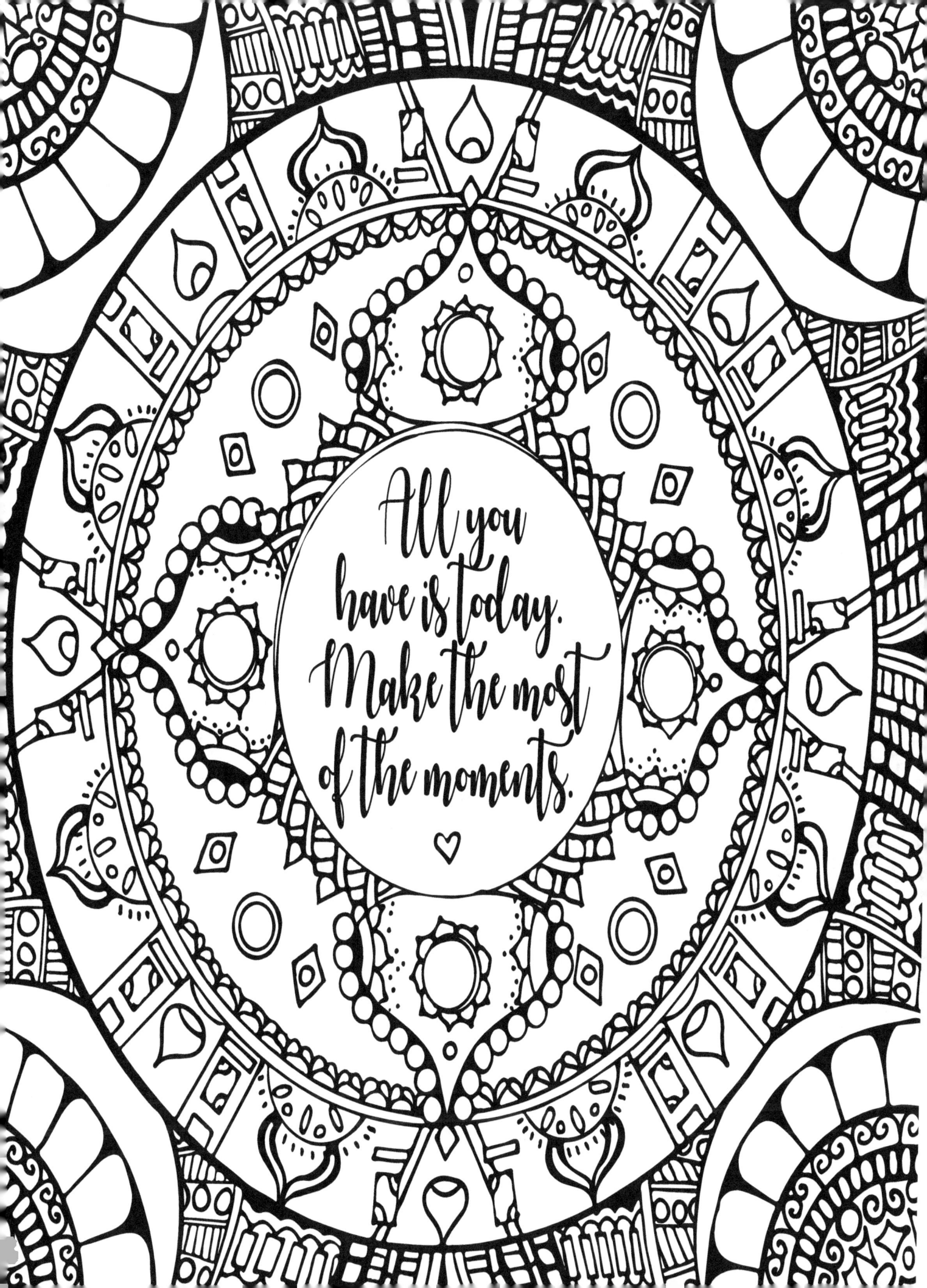

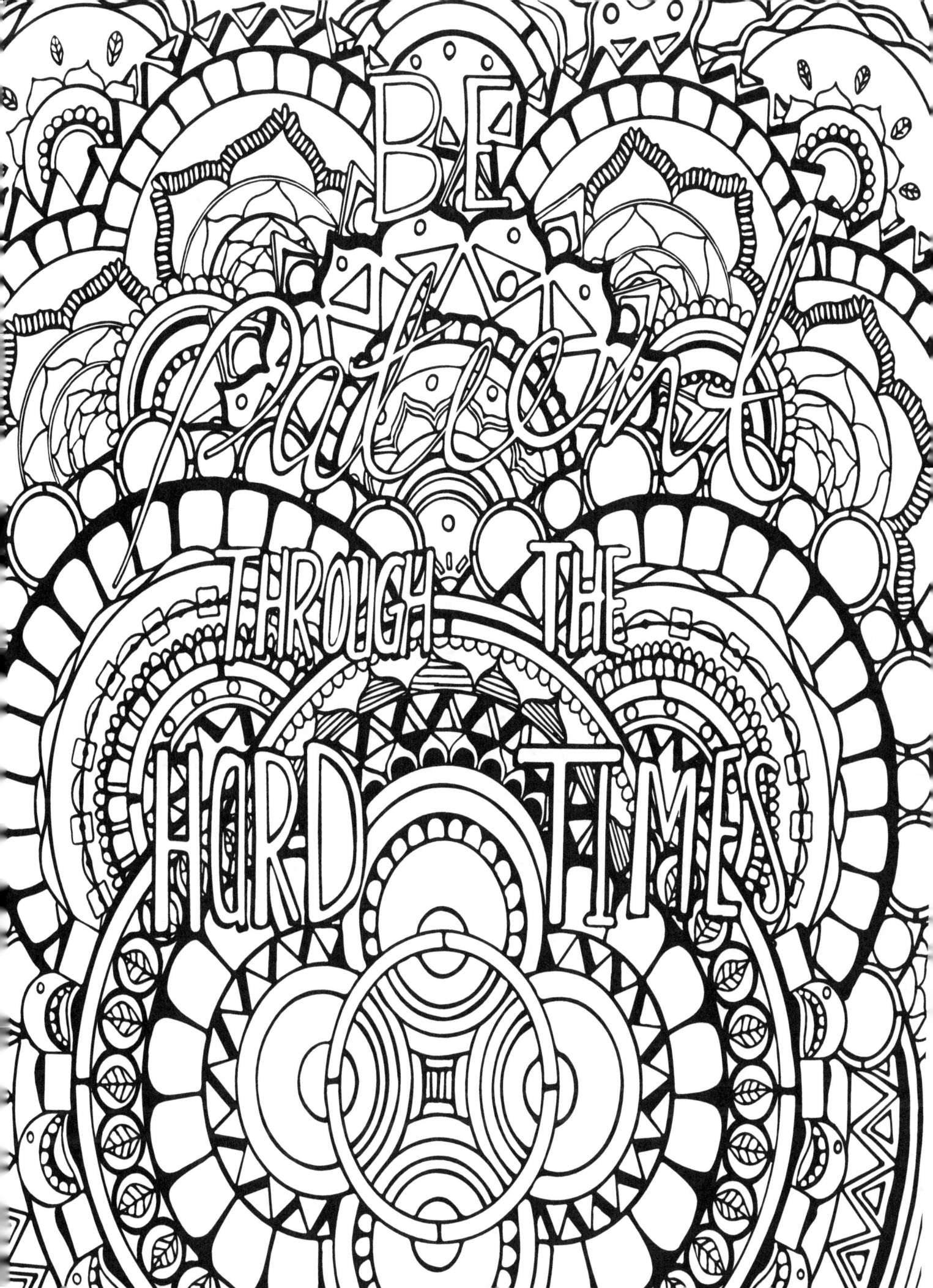

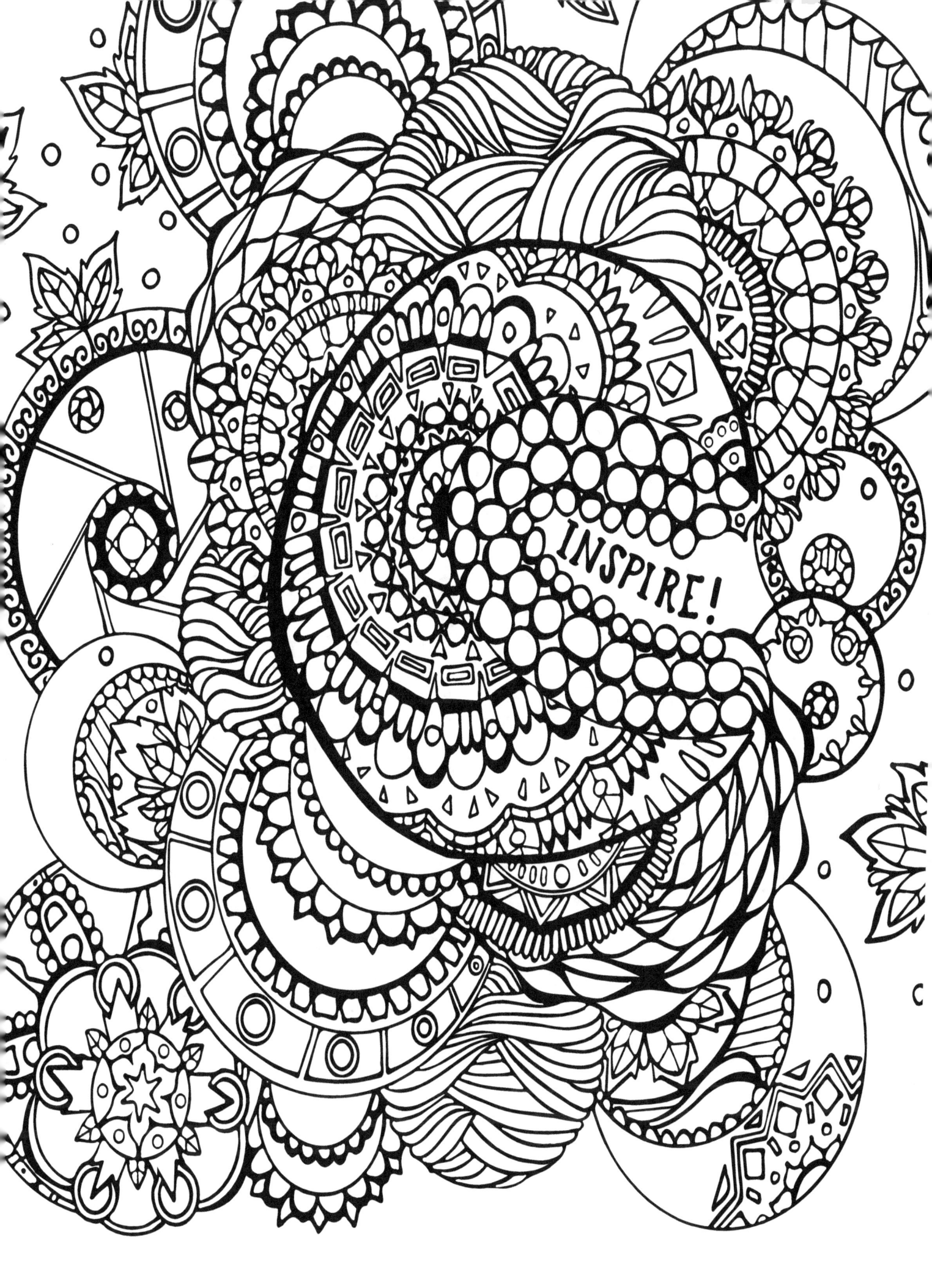

Best friends are the people in life that make you laugh a little louder, smile a little brighter, and live a little better.

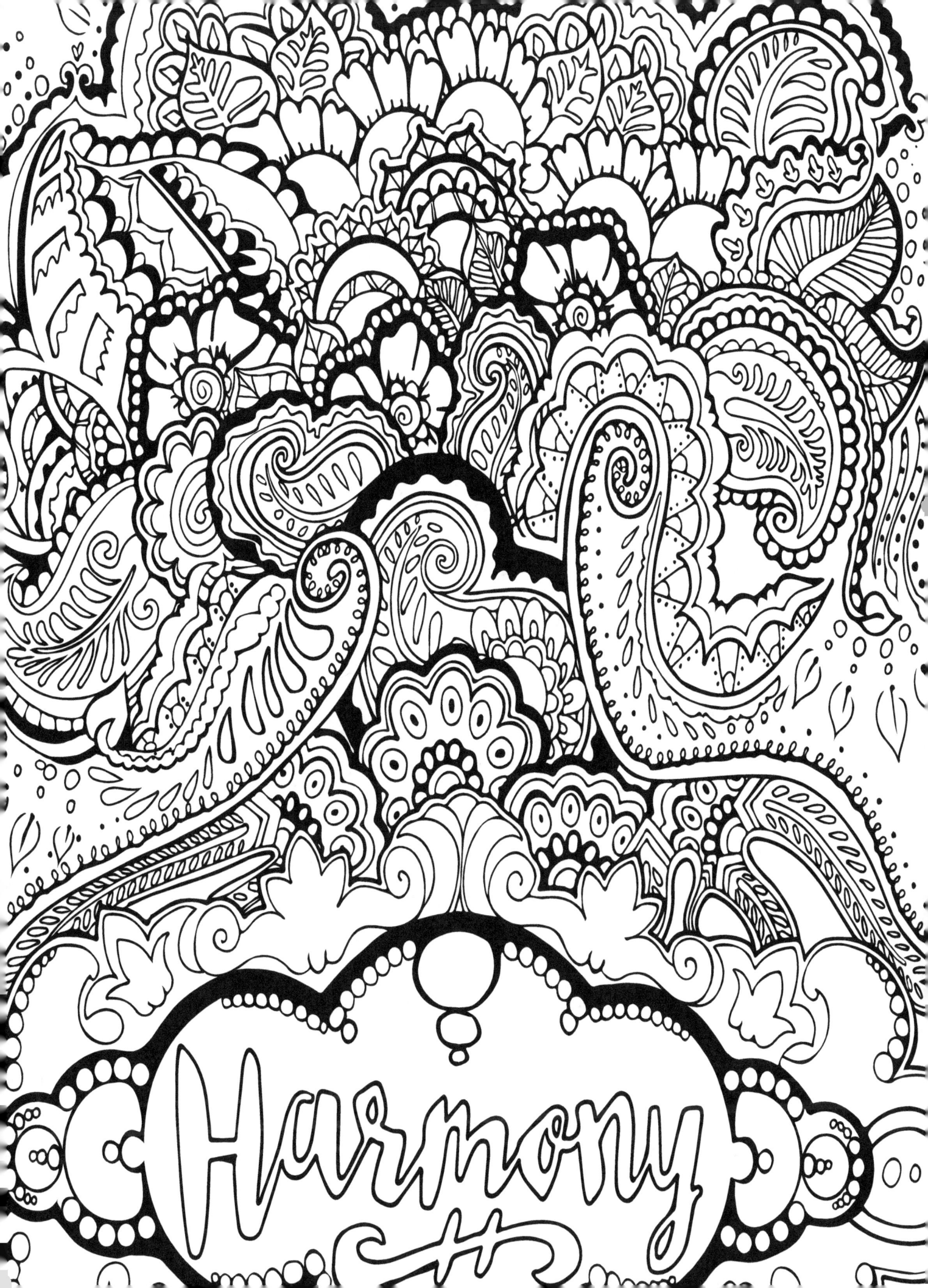

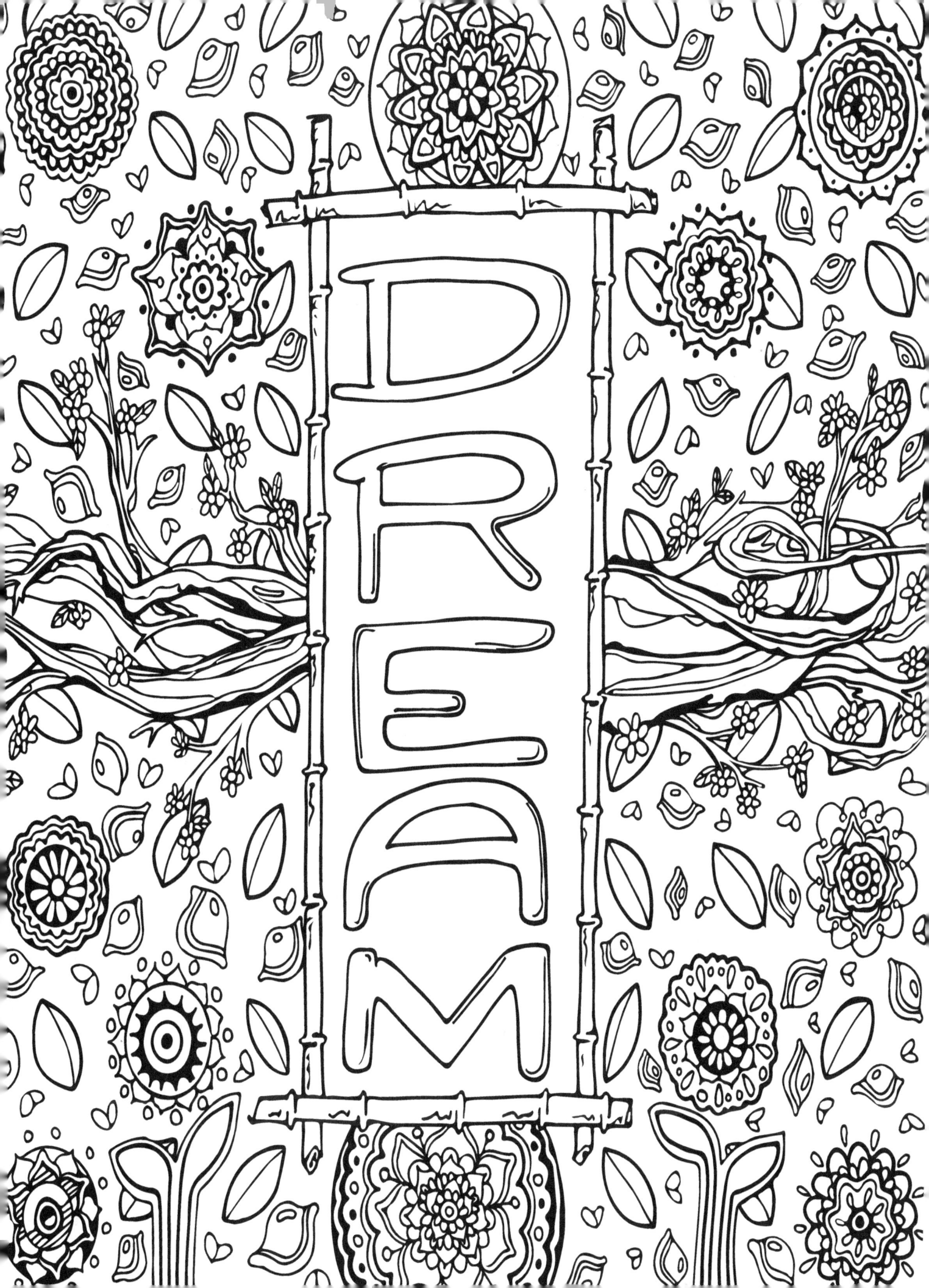

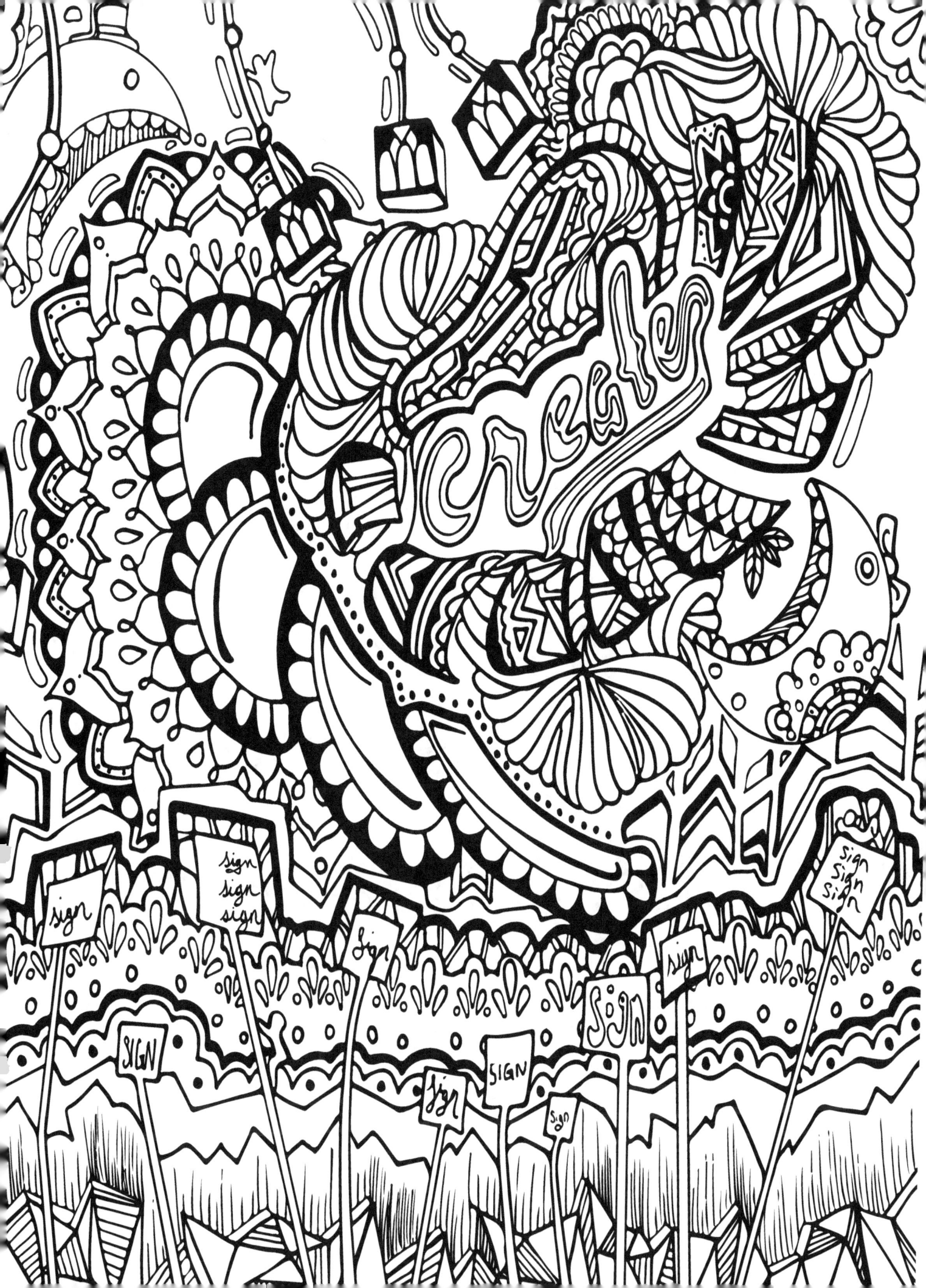

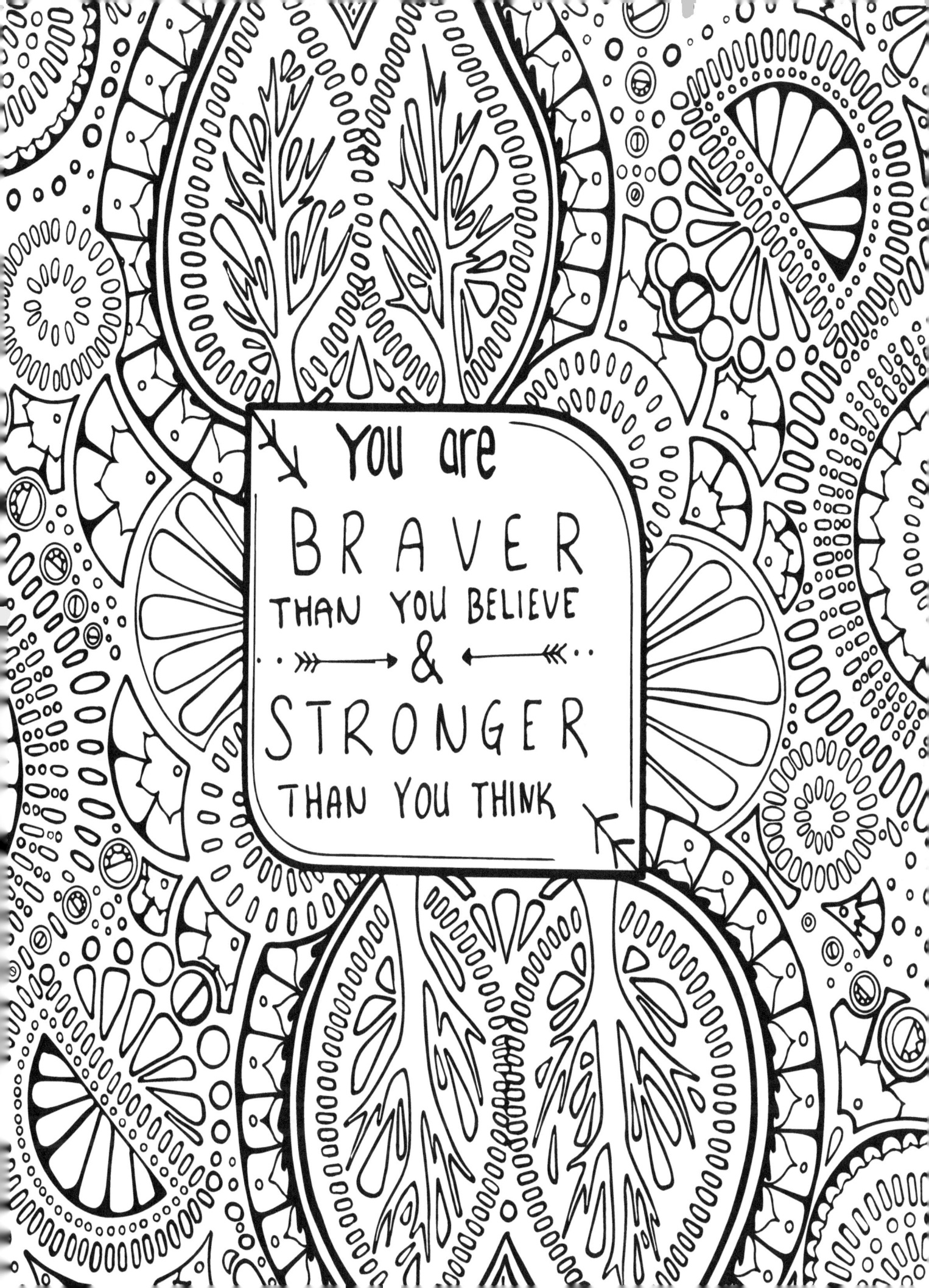

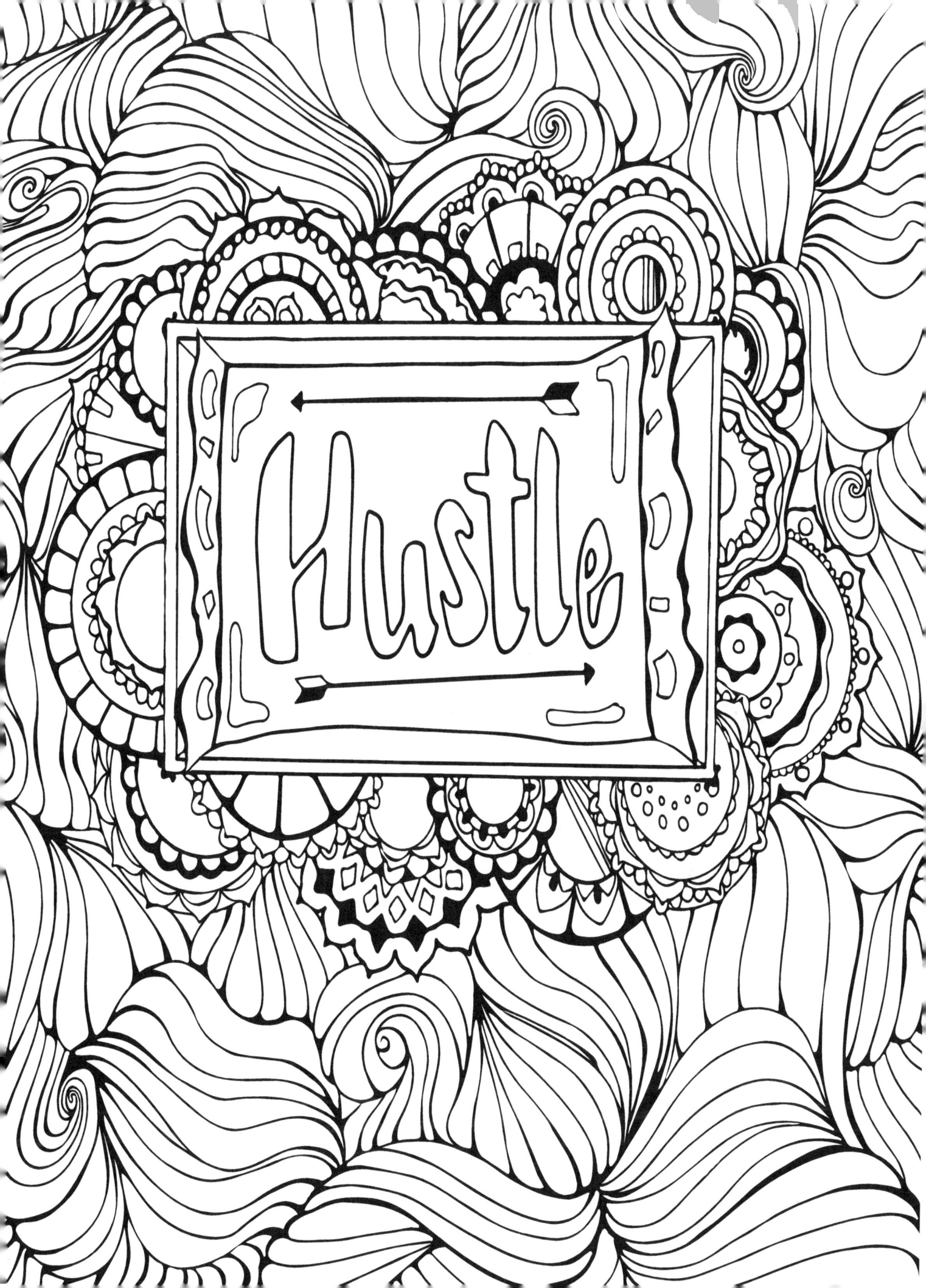

The only person you should try to be better than... is the person you were Yesterday.

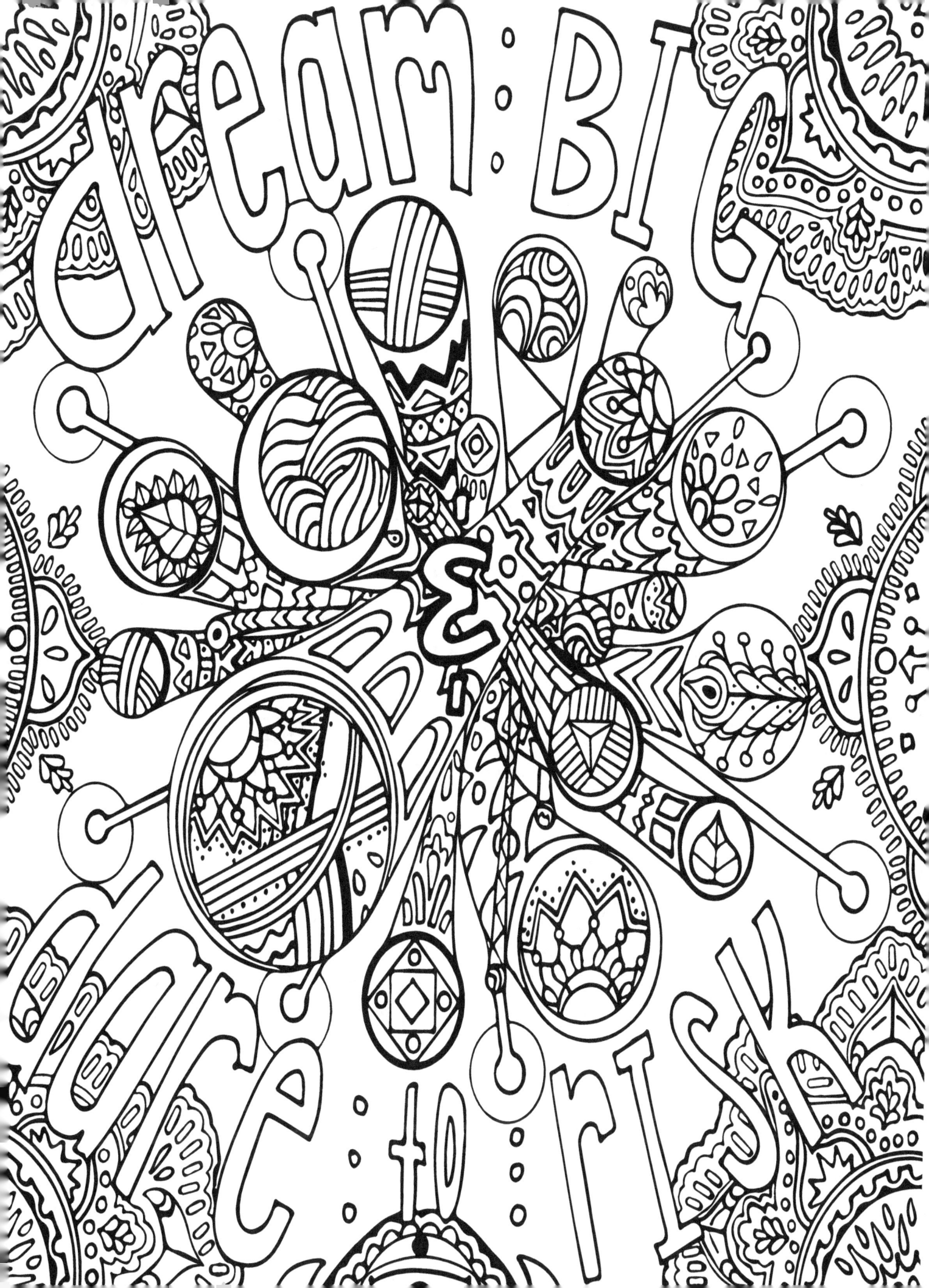

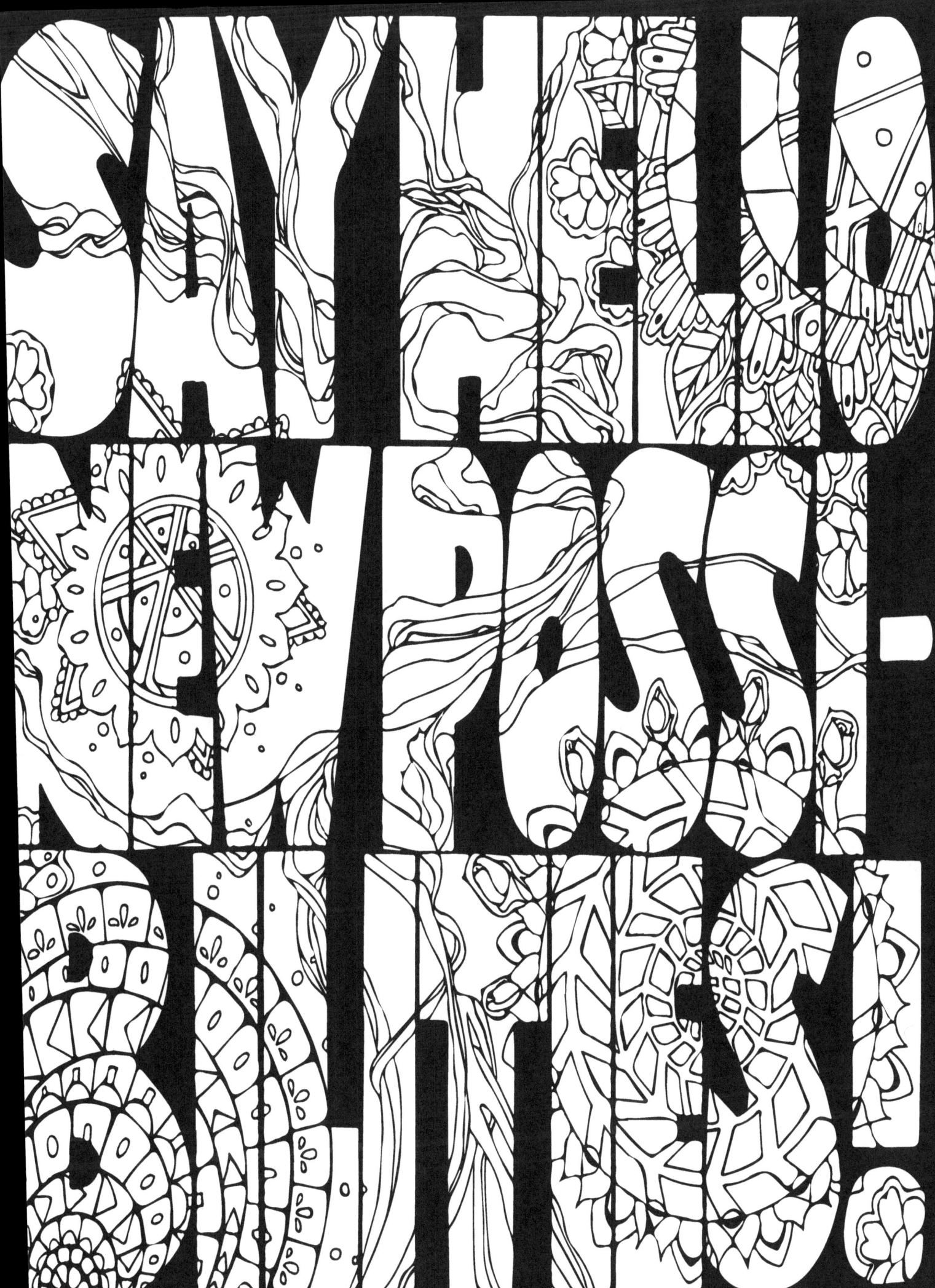

www.ingramcontent.com/pod-product-compliance
Lightning Source LLC
Chambersburg PA
CBHW062158220526
45470CB00009B/2856